PASSAGES IN THE LIFE OF A BUFFALO

by

Tyson Wallace

DUST [keep moving]

Constantly wretched

Wreck-ed

Sickest of guts and the filthiest of thoughts

Lost

Lost

Lust

Fuck or be fucked

Let's collect some dust

Down on bended knee

Down on bent, broken knees

Bloodied, smiling

Beaten, content

Diseased, silent

Rest assured it takes a man to be absurd

A bird to gather worms

A pig to chew the fat

Let's collect some dust

On our withered, broken backs

HOUNDS

I followed every cardinal rule

I followed the cardinal as he flew

Into the burning sun with his wings outstretched

Catching fire with hopes to clear his head

I'd rather be full of smoke than full of regret

Where will we fly when there's nowhere left to roam?

Carry me home on vulture's wings

There will be no telling what hell they'll bring

When the hounds cry into eternity

PHOENIX [creation from destruction]

Bottles on bottles

Beaches of discarded ash

The future is bright

THE CURE FEEDS THE DISEASE

Poison beckons poison beckons poison

Drugs requiring drugs requiring drugs

Cursed to speaking tongues, I'm speaking cursive

Tongue tied with after tastes of former loves

Poison beckons poison beckons poison

Drugs requiring drugs requiring drugs

Left inside the light attempting fire

Dimly lit and cold despite the sun

Poison beckons poison beckons poison

Drugs requiring drugs requiring drugs

BIRDS WITHOUT FLIGHT

Amidst weather for ducks I ate a murder of crows while the vultures picked my bones

I plucked tears from the Harlot's eyes because I can't sleep alone

I beg she doesn't fracture

I beg she doesn't break

Beneath the weight of a heavy heart and my bourbon pickled brain

"Can you hear them calling?" as the vultures start to screech

Carry me off to slumber on a mass of broken wings

ETERNAL LIFE [the curse]

I knew a guy who knew a guy

Who stuck a needle in his eye

He crossed his heart and hoped to die yet, wound up with eternal life

Life can be a bitch sometimes but, she might be easier to deal with if you didn't call her that, anyway….

I woke up with a headache again

I've forgotten how to ride my bike and I can't remember what it's like to relax

If you want if you can have it back, let's be honest I probably ruined it anyway

My liver hurts and my bones are tired and it's been so long since I've been inspired

If I find the time I'll crawl my way back home

Home alone and Satan sent

I can't afford to pay Hell's rent and Heaven seems to be all but, fucking vacant.

EDEN

Standing on shoulders of giants in the garden of Eden, picking the fruit from the trees

Standing on shoulders of giants in the garden of Eden, picking the fruit from my teeth

Where the serpent goes I'll follow Every slither, coil, and bend

My belly hurts with hunger The snake provides sweet medicine

The terrain out here is beautiful but it's wrought with sex and sin

Adam and Eve are inbreeding Fucking their next of kin

The serpent feeds me apples

Before the rats and worms they feed

on the rotten spoiled earth

left when the fruit falls from the trees

This world was born of waste

The wasted seed of earth and man

what kind of god would bare such fruit

just to call it forbidden?

now there's poison in the water

there's pollution in the skies

there's a preacher at the pulpit

retching fear and lies

While the rubies on his linens

start to lose their shine

the preacher lost his touch

now he's showing off his swine

So I released my snake at mass

he fed upon that pig

chewing on his sacrament

spewing bible verse and shit

the attendees barely noticed

Fanning the good book to beat the heat

All is all forgiven you can finally get some sleep

GLIMPSES

Acid on our tongues

The world opened wide for us

The other side waits

TAX SEASON

"Expect blood" he said

The only thing permanent

They always want blood

LEAP OF FAITH

Make time for the crash

Let your inhibitions go

Throw fear to the wind

DIALOGUE WITH DEATH

I exited the bar and made my way up the stairs to street level.

Standing there was a man in a black leather coat.

He struck a match using only the stubble on his jaw and proceeded to light a cigarette.

The man took a long drag, looked at me and smiled, then exhaled.

It was then that I knew who he was.

I looked at the man and I said, I said, "Death?" I said.

I said, "is it my time to go?"

Death took another drag and laughed deep from his belly and said "you don't understand son, you're already dead. We're ALL dead."

Then the sky opened up and the heavens spewed ashes across all the chimney tops

They set fire to our beds where we rested our heads and fucked 'til the sun came up

Then the sirens they sang, and the hounds came a calling spilling my guts in the streets

Chewing my insides, they quipped to each other "Man, these are pretty sweet eats."

MAN'S MAN [toxic masculinity]

He's nothing but a good batch of bad seed

a sharp wit and clean teeth

Forged from salted earth and chimney smoke

Cleans himself with a piece of steel and a well-oiled whet stone

He has scales for skin and a silver tongue that he polishes with bone

Some call him mud

Some call him sin

They suck him down like medicine

The rumors say that Satan hides from him

With poisoned wells, full of ants for eyes

and a face you'd just might recognize

on the off chance that you too, weren't born alive

When he arrives you can smell the drink

You can get drunk off his armpit stink

He's 200 proof and all the ladies love him neat

He'll spoil your guts and crack your bones

But he still beats going home alone

Even just for use of his swollen meat

COITAL BLISS

We heard the Devil's laughter

After we embraced in

the interior of hellfire

cue eye contact cue empty promises

wipe the seed away

wipe the sweat from your brow

There will be no breeding today

We've failed biology for pleasure

Hit me with that dopamine again

This is pure, un-cut oxytocin

Dealt from the hooves of God herself

This is Passion

This is a life of regret

This is vaginal comfort at its very best

It's warm like home in there

Disregard her heart

We'll deal with the consequences later

We can hide the scars

Every sticky fumbling

Every carnal thought

Every silly suck and fuck

Paves the way to a new lie

A new manipulation

A beautiful way to use and be used

Just don't forget to say I love you.

HOLY SPIRITS

Pickle my liver

Tear the light from my soul

load me up with alcohol and leave me alone

I force fed my conscience

I begged him for drink

The spirits gave my head a break but I can't help but think

That the bones in the water

Shed the light on the hole

That I continue to fill with things that damage my soul

Splinter my reality

Make it easy to tolerate the ugliness

I can't help but see.

MEAT

I've chewed the meat

I've swallowed the fat

Passed the beast through the valves of my heart

If counting the sheep

Can't bring any sleep

I want his wool and his meat

PASSION

Please don't bite your nails

I like the scratches that you leave

See? Dig into me

GOD ON SALE

Don't look now, there's a mob of monsters at your door

Wearing designer suits and wielding gospel as a weapon.

I can offer you salvation for the low low price of a wasted life

and a small fraction of your income, just to show his omnipotence

just how much you really care.

What exactly is the most popular currency in heaven? is it the

dollar? the euro? the yen? No matter the country of origin fear

is the business, god damn it's good business. Raking in the cash

faster than they can spill the guilt.

The confessional is still warm.

More ears than a cornfield have heard of your sins.

I guess god too has loose lips.

Your secrets are safe with me but it comes with a fee.

Amen.

ILLUSION OF FREEDOM [The maze of addiction]

Intoxicated

Intoxicated but free

At least I feel free...

SELF-[destruct]MEDICATE

Drink relax enjoy

Let anxiety take you

The panic is yours

BEAST AMONGST MEN [disguised as spirit] I am not a man

I am but skeleton

Painted in flesh

With booze for blood

And shit for a grin

Much to my chagrin

I'm alive

I'm alive

I'm alive

Bring me some medicine

I'm sick, Oh so sick

A flaccid man with a flaccid prick

Sick sick six

Sick six six

Six six six

The only beast here is me

BUTTON PUSHER

I fanned the flames to boil your blood

And scorched my flesh with the iron

I admire your wit but once the words are writ they can't quite be forgotten

When your bones start to splinter

I'll pick up the pieces and tuck them away in my skin

Skeletal and smiling, from all the medicine

VULNERABILITY [move on]

Wipe the spill with your sleeve

Watch the crimson spread through the fibers like forest fire

Taste the iron on your tongue

Unclench your jaw

Don't forget to breathe

What's done is done

No crying over spilt milk

Spilled blood

Soiled silk

Lost love

Wipe your heart from your sleeve

FLAWED [beauty in the broken]

Quiet your mind

Spill your guts

Kill your past

Slip away darling

Don't live untouched

Unwashed

Un-bloomed

There's wretch in the cleanliness

There's a place for love

And it's not here

So odd

So queer

So debonair

Refuse eternity

Refuse the Everlasting

Own thy disrepair

DRINK FOR SPORT [a cry for acceptance]

I think one more beer will do

Not leaving this room until my fingernails embed the floor

I'll walk out with a little less teeth and a smile on my face

An ode to a Friday night

THE MAJORITY [no one's getting out alive]

Sing songs of the damned

Surely they will hear your cries

Damned rule in numbers

SENSES [the most underappreciated gifts]

Hands can be eyes too

With the perfect set of drugs

Touch taste hear smell see

DNA [you are art]

Do you see the red?

It's spilling through the canvas

There's art in your blood

WORTH OF ROCKS

We fucked to the beat of gunshot

We came to the sounds of their screams

For the utter disregard of good measure

In ratios of inch to miles

All smiles toward the destruction that surrounded our passion

Blood

Sweat

Tears

Semen

It didn't matter which was which

She drank it in goblets on the corner of Massacre and Fuck street

Where she made her first dollar

Where she made her abortion proud to be home

The procedure lasted longer than the ring on her finger

I guess diamonds aren't forever either

Mistakes measured in rocks

In a pretty velvet box

That shares the same worth as the latex we send beneath the city

Wash your bastards away

Dimwitted swimmers will just disappoint us anyway

Who said I had the right to be the sperm that won the race?

PAPER THIEF

Unguarded guardian

Take a walk on the wild side

Let down your guard

Split sides from false hope and reside only where it's comfortable

Nowhere more

No less than the illusion of progress

The ever so tedious process of the downward spiral

Today is the day and it's slipping away

With every tick, every tock

I'll take the walk knowing all the while it carries only the permanence of a cigarette

Inhale

Breath gloom

Try not to catch flu

Yellow grins and whiskey spins pave the way to our futures

and I'm laughing all the way

D

  O

    W

     N

      .

      .

      .

      .

      .

      .

OVERCOME [fight for the light]

Give way to the gloom

Let the gray wash over you

There is a stillness in the cold

There is a calmness in the fog

Embrace the damp

Take in the darkness

Never mind the sun

MOVE FORWARD

Uncertainty is a hell of a drug

Quite the crippling one in fact

More addictive than heroin

More accessible than air

It'll kill you quick and leave you asking for more death

Decide

INDIVIDUALISM [no one has your same bones]

Remain skeletal in your demeanor

Never show your skin

They will scar you if you let them

Wear your bones proudly

Speak in tongues

Take his name in vain

Shed your skin

SLUMBER

Show me a place to hide my shadows

My cup runneth o'er with skeletons

Show me a place to store my sorrow

So I can learn to sleep again

SCARECROW

Now cursed with a brain The Scarecrow begs for fire

Cigarette in hand, stuffed full of straw and regret

toward the loss of blissful ignorance

Now cursed with a brain The Scarecrow doesn't sleep.

His mind races through the night wondering when it all changed.

His life used to be full of color and song and yellow brick roads.

Now it's full of gray and panic and little yellow pills.

Just to take the edge off, just to quiet his mind.

The mind he begged and battled witches for.

Sure, it wasn't always great

It was violent and full of flame and flying primates,

but at the time he was too stupid to know any better.

Now cursed with a brain he wants to give it all back.

To forget.

He would give anything to forget.

How about a little fire, Scarecrow?

BURGUNDY RAIN

There's something not quite right with the scenery

Nothing here seems familiar to me at all

The hills have grown eyes

The trees sprouted tusks

The concrete is screaming at the top if it's lungs

The humans are panicking

Begging for grace

While the defeated preacher preaches that it's too late

Bury your guns

Hide your head in the sand

Before the asphalt wakes up and starts feeding again

The skies spilling fire

Spread by poisonous winds

While the clouds slit their wrists to get one last rain in

I bathed in the warmth of the red from the skies

Oceans of rubies poured from pillowy white

'Til the ground opened up and started to bite

Being caught in the rain almost made me feel alive

HABITS

Too many beers

Too many cigarettes

I have a headache that feels closer to home than I've been in a long time.

The music was great tonight, I can't say the same about the company.

I'm dehydrated

My veins are protruding

I have a sick pain in my guts

It's 3:26 and I'm alone again

The TV is on

I wish I could remember what sleep was like

Maybe one more beer

Maybe one more cigarette

BUS STOP: 'EARTH'

I'd surely kill for a place to sit

My feet are tired and my lips are split

from the cold dry air and too many cigarettes

There was water here it used to flow

Just like you and me rivers too get old

When did this place lose all its majesty?

It was raped for oil and fresh spilt blood

What was once called earth we now call mud

The grandest of all burial plots

BLUE LIGHT

Sight in the darkness

Doth occur with chemicals

place this on your tongue

ADMISSION

I drink from breakfast to bedtime

yet I haven't been drunk in months times nine.

Is that a problem?

I spend more on booze than I do food

And I've forgotten what it's like to be 22

Is that a problem?

I've got broken bones and scarred up skin

Just so I can abuse medicine

Is that a problem?

I've burnt bridges with made up fires

And I'm the one who calls out "Liar!"

Is that a problem?

I help you search for the shit I stole

And I conjure shit that you swallow whole

Because the drugs they make me good at speaking woe

Is that a problem?

I've got scotch for blood and a smoke-filled head

And I won't feel full until I'm dead.

Is that a problem?

I've counted coins and I've sold my seed

For another drink or a bag of weed

But I still can't seem to get a wink of sleep.

Is that a problem?

Do I have a problem?

I think I have a problem....

LION MAN

Nothing quite like time well wasted

Chopped up and pasted

Like a page torn from a book

Cluttered and dust-ridden

Yet I'm forbidden to read the words it bears

Complete with pointed fingers and uncomfortable stares

Uncharted and haunted and phobic of spaces

I'll wander the streets on a cloud

Precipitating and passing out horror

Acting as a product of an environment I created

Feeling comfort in my ill conceived justifications

All the while knowing what I'm doing is wrong

I am the one true love you'll never meet

I am the roller coaster

I am the liar

I am the lion man

King of the beasts

Feeling carnivorous

Intoxicating the streets

ERASER/ERASURE

Eraser

Eraser

Un-doer

My maker

Help me erase the errors

The many errors of my ways

Erasure

Erasure

I've been cleansed of every thought

All thought of hope, you've found me out

Thoughtless but careful

I swear now I'll be careful

The eraser doth provide new avenues for denial

Never mind the cover up I will be reborn

Eraser

Eraser

A Baptist

The Savior of the wicked and the wanted

Pull my body from the river and see how well my former sins can swim.

A clean slate from soiled lakesAll our sins have been erased

Eraser

Eraser

My scapegoat and savior

Erasure

Erasure

There is grandeur in the errors of your ways.

BURNT FLESH

"Don't tread too far" The lonesome gentleman said

Are you full of liquor or are you full of regret?

We're counting bodies because the sheep are all dead

I've been fed but I'll never feel full

Upon a canvas of stretched fat and sinew

I will forge my name

Strike the iron while the iron is hot

only the metal will then be to blame

there are no lies inside the brand

the smell will cease as will the heat

this is survival now

who will wear my brand?

bear my name and shed your flesh

so tonight I can eat meat

BAPTIST'S WIT

Last call for redemption

The confessional's closed

I bartered with the wisemen

In Lucifer's clothes

Whether God or the Devil

All fairy tales must come to an end

Either sing with the choir

Or die in the sand

Let us dance in the fire

While we practice our Baptist's wit

It was a real nice writ

But the thought makes me sick

Pay your dues

Pay your tithes

Feel it tighten

That rope of guilt 'round your neck

Sing the songs

Bow your head

Read your scripture

Hold your breath

Hold on tight

This is it

SNORT OF VENOM

Such a pretty pity

We've been partying all night

Everybody's playing victim

Everybody's packing knives

All the guests are in their best dress

Donning silk to hide their scales

I love the way they slink and slither

With forked tongues flecking tall tales

They shudder in excitement

I see the venom on their lips

I could fill a snifter

If I could only catch the drips

I can hear their conversations

I can see their stares and grins

"How do you suppose it is they sleep

while wearing all that skin"?

FEED

As of late I've been drinking too much and sleeping far too little

I wonder if one has to do with the other?

I'm sure it's no coincidence

I just can't pinpoint the moment where it all started

The chicken or the egg

Insomnia or drink

Neuroses feeding addiction feeding neuroses

The real question is, which will be the death of me?

I'm sure only time can tell now but my money's on the drink

For death may finally bring blessed sleep

But not today

Today I remain awake....

...and smiling.

KILLING TIME [til it kills me]

I count my spoils making tick marks on my hooves

I measure time in cigarettes and the blues

The type of blues you can't help but sing when it rains

Counting the drops until the sky falls down again

THE EXIT [change ain't easy]

Jagged and splintered

The break isn't always clean

Take pride in your shards

DANCE AWAY

We danced the dance of decadence

Incognito

For the sake of being stubborn

Like a dying wish

A final breath

The dance

Quarter turn

Take a bow

End scene

Fade out

Keep a smile and a steady pace

Keep a firm right hand

Lest you lose sight of your dying wish

Dance

HINDSIGHT [some things you can't take back]

The dunce cap is mine!

I came by it fashionably

She bleeds me dry

I dance macabre and aggravated

I came on high to bring hardship to the streets

With reddened fists

And the blood of angels on my teeth

Take heed the warning

The dunce cap is mine!

TREAD

Whether soil or solitude

We all need room to grow

Where there's war there is blood

All the wolves drinking blood

Whether cancer or cavity

Decay too tends to grow

Where he treads there is Mud

Let us all turn to Mud

RED, WHITE, AND BLUES

You don't see ants killing ants or punching through drywall

And we're supposed to be the superior being?

Flies: they eat shit and get trapped by our windows

Yet we get caught in traps we've constructed ourselves

Paper, cloth, plastic, electricity

So far gone from the barest necessities, clear cut naivety

Living each day for some lust driven form of brand-new machinery

I'll give you a dollar if you slit your wrists

Insurance will cover it, "you've got a deal mister!"

If I bleed to death, I just don't give a shit

So long as my bank account leaves an impressive number behind

I'll go to the grave with a twelve-carat diamond watch

A nice fucking suit and a heart full of slander

Leaving my children with bruised broken hearts

I was too busy to give them attention

These dead presidents that are printed on cotton

They far outweigh all my own flesh and bone

 Blow off the kids for too many square feet

That I can call my very own broken home

Love all thy neighbors and fuck all the rest

"God Bless America?" genocide says it best

Children are starving "but it's so far away"

Enjoy your meal, have a great fucking day

Red white and blue? More like blood cum and lithium

Your prescriptions expired good luck with your detox

The American dream

LYCANTHROPE

A Silver tongue and several severed smiles

intoxicated the she-wolf that lives under the marquis

The creatures saw and quickly grew restless

The monsters all seem bored

They've grown tired of the drugs they sought

They've lost their taste for whores

So they wait under the marquis

Striking self conscious poses

Twiddling their claws and picking their fangs

Waiting for a full moon or a silver bullet

What makes a man a monster

Just might make a monster man

SWINE

Boys will be boys

Pigs will be pigs

As sure as crows making murder

Alongside the bridge

Boys will be piggish

For God made man from swine

Born in his image

Turning flesh into rind

As long as there's slop

Man will surely stay fed

Gnashing their teeth

Against the tusks of their dead

I swear by my snout

And the curl of my tail

Pigs need a God

Like the winds need a sail

Boys will be boys

Pigs will be pigs

Gods would be gods

If they could only exist

STARDUST

I was cut from the stars

Carved from infinity

Molded, iron by iron

Carbon by carbon

By sands of time and winds of happenstance

An electro magnet in a meat suit, complete with an ego and an ignorant grin.

A mass of flesh and fur and teeth.

A mess

A man

A mannequin

Forged from chaos and stardust

Filled with lust and depression

Send me home

Send me back to the stars

Send me back to atoms on the winds of nuclear fire

Give me the energy to exist.

LOVE/HATE LOVE DRUGS

There's no room for the grace of god when you bask in self-destruction

I saw red before it all when black and I woke up wearing crimson

The taste of iron and alcohol tears me back into existence

Fuck me up

Feed me drugs

Tell me that this is love

Pile the bricks

Build your walls

I'll be fine with alcohol

Fuck me up

Feed me drugs

I just hope the drugs can bring me love

THE DIVINE MAN

Piss and vinegar

Coursing through the veins of God

Proof we're made from him

SENSORY DEPRIVATION [always be grateful]

Cataracts are gifts

When there's nothing left to see

Embrace the blindness

SELF SABOTAGE

Follow the shatter

Give way to the break

Trust in destruction

Lest the birds seal your fate

We counted the lambs

Picking chops from our teeth

While we begged for our widows to cry us to sleep

Under cover of darkness

I tried to recreate light

Whilst I smothered the candles

Trying to pick a fight

I said goodnight to the spoils

I pushed slumber away

Praying for shut eye

With eyelids taped to my face

SCARS

"Feed your head" the handsome gentleman said

to the man in his burial suit

lack of slumber has me feeling strange

is the booze to blame?

or should I just admit my brain is broke

have another smoke

Walk it off

Eat the hair from the dog

There's no god here

there's never been

you smell of sin

Show me your skin

I beg of you show me your skin

TRUTH [the great desalinator]

I lost control of my body at seaside amongst sands of shattered glass reflecting a dying sun

the locals were shivering in the heat while the tourists counted their spoils

and documented their triumphs in digital view while the recipients remained blind as bats

the waves were deafening as they crashed with the force of the misery of every man woman and child lost at sea

you could still smell the blood when the tide came in, there was sorrow in the mist reminiscent of a crooked neck or a carved wrist

I overheard a child asking his mother why the ocean was so salty, to which she responded. "there's a grain of salt for every lie ever told in that water. Before mankind came along you could drink from the oceans."

MINIMUM WAGE

Your bones for your wage

For sacrifice of body

The bills will get paid

DRIFT ON

take heed the warning for the reckoning comes late tonight

the moon is high and our bellies are full of meat

don't retreat into the darkness

don't spoil the spoils

don't ignore the spirits that burn your esophagus and insulate your bones

you are not alone, there's chaos in such numbers

there's a wreck inside the mass

no leaves no grass no greenery

just oceans made of ash

take heed

feed your head or feed the machine

pay your tolls from the hospital bed

repentance is useless until you're brave enough to die

so salvage a ticket and proceed with the ride

I bartered with god for mine

 all it cost was my life

spill your blood to cross the velvet rope

I'll see you inside

I'd save you a seat for the sake of good form

but there's a thing about hell you see.

the seats are always warm

BUGS

We've always assumed insects are stupid for making an early exit.
Even with 24 hour life spans, we find them dead in the dumbest of
ways and places. In our drinks, dried out and shriveled in masses
on our radiators. Flying toward light fixtures and bug zappers as
if suicide was redemption. An entire species of kamikazes. What
if we're the stupid ones? What if the insects know something we
don't? What if humans are the only species that fight to survive
this plane of existence? Hospital beds, multi-vitamins, anti-
biotics, anti-smoking ads, so many tools to delay the inevitable,
and for what? A bigger house, a better car, green printed cotton?
No matter where you travel the sky is still the same. The insects
are bumping themselves off left and right. Maybe it's time for
humanity to take note.

THE BURIAL [a memento mori]

Pile on the dirt

Here lies life reduced to rot

Baptized by the dirt

DON'T GIVE UP [you are not alone]

Disenfranchised youth

Ever growing in numbers

Your time is coming

ADAPT

Smoke but no papers

Already one of those days

Good morning karma

CHEMICAL FIX [you're making me sick]

It gets easier

With prescription ignorance

Swallow down a smile

BREAK THE CYCLE

Where did I go wrong?

The curse of infinity

A sentence to hell

TIME LOOP

Another day lost

To insomnia and drink

Bring me death or sleep

LOSS FOR WORDS

I can hurt myself better than you can just for the sake of competition

And baby, I'm winning

I've become a walking cliché with a running nose

And a pointless vendetta with a bottle in hand and a nervous smile

I'm a man about vices [and I bear them proudly]

Ain't a blanket quite like excess

Especially for the purposes of smothering

And it's warmer in there than I've been in a long time

Yet still not fulfilled 'til I get my fill

I think I'll take another pull spend another night on the rocks

With the heartburn to remind me that it's still beating

And I'll keep retreating with a fake god complex that rivals the Greeks

Without my Aphrodite

Holding on to a sarcastic swagger that holds no meaning

No purpose but an agenda like that of a parasite

But the host died a long time ago

Rotting and corroded like the ship I sailed along endless seas of bourbon

When I knew all along that surely there was no destination worth heading to

Beyond the horizon

But I dare not waste a second of time thinking

[Especially in regard to ifs, ands, or buts.]

BUT/AND/IF I could think of and honest adjective to justify my means

I'd use it readily

But I'm at a loss for words.........

CULT CLASSICK

I look at life on Earth and all I see is a suicide cult. An entire

species drowning in a trough of time pissed away. No matter your job,

no matter your income, no matter your appearance, we're all just

killing time until killing season. Rather than a noose or a gun,

the majority of us take the long route, death by a thousand cuts.

One more burger, one more hit, one more drink, one more silly suck

and fuck. What's on TV? Where did the time go? Fill my glass.

Set me up. An endless cycle of destruction to pass a man-made construct.

Let me pass the time with the rest of the flock. Racing toward

the inevitable while fearing a fake god and the feeling of cold

ground, yet we continue to run to the ground. I joined a suicide

cult today. This day of my birth, the race has begun. I hear I'll

get my name today, I'll start my journey toward the end. I joined

a suicide cult today.

We are the homo-sapiens and we have a life to waste.

AMPERSANDS

Sloth like a sunset

Lay my body to the west

Soon after you'll find that uncharted waters are better kept at that

So keep your hands to yourself

and I'll keep mine nicotine stained and callous aplenty

When you realize you no longer have the world at your fingertips

I'll gladly remove mine from your throat

So now you know that wherever you go

I'll have a part of you, and you'll have a piece of me

And when the bile corrodes

I'll chew my own skin

To turn my insides out

Frolic about in the wilderness we created

Dancing and fucking upon God's tired stage

And when the audience boos we'll break out in laughter

Burn the coliseum to the ground

Then when we're admitted

Better yet, committed, and we're eating our meals through a tube

I'll take it all in with a gluttonous smile

All the while I'll be thinking of truth

Truth of life and human err

Distort the fairest of fair beyond all repair

We can only feel nothing but good

HAPPY FACE

The end is near I'm going out with a shot in my stomach

The flag on our ship's at half-mast and we haven't the slightest sense of direction

We lost all concept of time long ago and I think we're crashing

Hats off to our modern-day heroes who inspire our thoughts and ideals

"Cut your hair, read a book, make a difference" be happy in arrogance

You're all just a fish out of water when there isn't a pond

A parasite with no host just a copy of a clone

The world record for longest living is skipping

And you haven't a place to call home

The flocks the masses, stacked like books of matches

Our guests are getting distracted

The sheep are getting distracted

Drink up be merry cheers everyone in the room

Oh god we could have it all

My god we could have it all

So let's fuck, take drugs, pretend that we're in love

It'll only last if you ignore it

Put on a happy face

Put on a happy face

BLACK COFFEE [inspired by the artwork of Reese Dillon Wallace]

I don't understand young people anymore.

I don't dislike them, I just don't understand them.

They're all in such a big damn hurry to grow up, and the men don't respect the

women. It makes me want to stretch out the skin on my throat and yank my flaccid

prick as I yell out: "This is what you're racing toward, right here! Now get off

your phone and pay attention to that beauty, she's not going to be interested

in you forever!"

I want to but I don't.

I just sit and watch.

At least the coffee is good.

Coffee I understand.

It's strong, simple, quick to conjure a memory.

Many of my life's most important memories, good or ill are associated with

black coffee in one way or another.

"Can I get you some cream for your coffee?" She asked, topping off my cup.

"No thank you, dear." I smiled.

She seemed annoyed as she walked away.

I guess they don't understand me either.

SILVER LININGS

You can find me in the murk and the mold

You can find me in the wood where virus grows

You can find me in the haunted house

With the witches and the ghosts

Where the spirits reign from bottles in the soot

Holy ghosts

From holy hell

Pull filthy thoughts

From poisoned wells

And sit in stink of sulfur pulled from hell

You can find me in the barrel with the brew

You can find me in the graveyard stealing boots

You can find me in the heavens being banished

By St. Peter and his minions, pitching woo

Put pennies on my eyes to pay the tolls

I will pay my penance to the trolls

I will earn my dues with all the monsters

I will send my love to all the ghouls

You can Find me in the soil with the roots

You can find me with the devils under hoof

You can find me in the fire with my peers

At very best or very worst

At least it's warm in here

ODE TO S. MUNDI

I saw god last night

in perfect geometry

She was beautiful

TWO LEFT FEET

I can't help but feeling that I feel nothing and that's fine

If what you're preaching is "something's wrong" then you're right

I could start dancing, but both my feet have grown left

I'd slay a man for the surety of rest

Every pill, every supplement is a warning

That there is something wrong with my head

the evidence is more than circumstantial

this earth we've grown into is pure hell

a warning bell

a pissing race

a plot of land

a resting place

a consequential bed of roses where the truth died

a box of secrets, lined with alcohol and lace

a wounded elder, liver spotted and unburdened

a child with a toothless smiling face

We built our homes upon hell

all is well

all is well

we built our homes and poisoned the well

all is well

all is well

WRECK

Don't look at me I'm drunk again

I know I broke my promise

But I'm just a man I beg you please forgive me

Look past my shortcomings

If I could afford the attire I'd be a wolf in sheep's clothing

But I'm broke and there's no disguising

My fangs, my coat, my thievery

I'm a wolf, I've always been

You can see flesh in my teeth When I force a grin

Flash a smile

Silver tongue

Silver bullets

Bring me love

Howling blind at the moon

Singing my song to you

But you're deaf from the wreck

The rotten wretched mess that I left when I left

Hear my howl

Hear my cry

Cut my wool

Much obliged

Feral men cannot get rest

I can't recall the last time I slept, I'm a mess

I'm a wolf

I'm everything but heaven sent the wolf has caused a wreck

INFINITE NOW [god is within]

The second coming

So many ignorant souls

There wasn't a first

THE GAME

A new generation of freaks have come to walk across the wire

Callous hands feed the gluttonous mouth of the whore that lives next door

Their minds confined by memories past and fairy tales, naive

Their smoke floats up like strands of hair

Their music increases in tone

These lives they lead

This stage they've built

They try to swallow whole

Yet again, they choke upon the thoughts of what's to come

A carnival of lust and psychedelia

Sex, drugs, and rock n roll

Spill your guts

Let's hear it

They're begging to be heard

Spell it out with a big Fuck you! and call it a Friday night

I think I've played this game before

There are no winners here my friend

There are no winners here

CHARMER

I traded my teeth for daggers

So, I could peel back your skin with my smile

You coughed up your heart to make room

And I charmed my way in

I poked and prodded your insides

When I should have been searching your mind

Now these daggers are harder to clean

I miss you like I miss my teeth

Out of reach

Out of turn

Out of line

Wine is fine

Blood is wine

Bleed me dry

Fill this cup for the audience

The guests, they're all starting to stare

My mouthful of knives shining bright

Reflecting the replicate swine

Brush my teeth with steel wool

Scrub the metal

Clean the blades that doth sever and trim

While you're off celebrating in grandeur

I'll be missing the taste of your skin

ATTENTION GRAB [love yourself first]

Nobody's hero

Nobody's aspiration

A blood cell in the heartbeat of the city

I'll keep you entertained

I'll feed you full

All the while I go hungry

A sheep amongst the wolves

Such a pretty little pig

Look at me! Look at me!

Such a busy little bee

Look at me! Look at me!

Unconscious masochist

Ungodly swine

Unclench your teeth and smile

While I shake my own death rattle

Pretty pretty please

Look at me! Look at me!

Pretty pretty please

Look at me! Look at me!

I'll be leaving soon I promise

And you won't lose a wink

You won't lose a second thought

Pondering over me

All I ask is

Look at me! Look at me!

Someone please Look at me! Look at me!

COST

For a low low price

You can try to exit life

Your loved ones will pay

CONSCIOUSNESS [make your own history]

I don't belong here

Where did my universe go?

I wish I could leave

EGO DEATH

With the thirst of Dionysus

And the lust of Aphrodite

I'll preach debauchery on every street corner

With a pack of Strikes and a bottle of spirit

Like it was written in the King James Bible

There's nothing decent about this exposure

The negatives are fried beyond recognition

No recollection of the night before

Save a nose bleed from a bad habit

Burning bridges before they're even constructed

My childhood dreams have split at the seams

And no one is impressed by my cries of distress

I confess I feel I've earned the right to be selfish

Unless you disagree but I won't give you the courtesy

The satisfaction

You've rubbed my ego raw

OBLIGED

On this cold night, fore winter's dawn

I sit alone, no hope, no song

I've watched the moon in wax and wane

With hopes to see your face again

I'll sit and dwell on memories past

Hold onto them until my breath's last

The liquid spills like April's showers

But it produces no May flowers

If my wrists should cut they'll call it love

The feel of hot, wet, sticky blood

If life should pass without a cue

I'll pass away in thought of you

I've never been one for goodbyes

For now I'll say "I'm much obliged"

I'll leave you now with my last words

"Don't cry for me, this shouldn't hurt"

OF FROG AND FLY

In the garden there were frogs that screamed over the flies they ate.

"No matter the flies." Father said, "They feed and they feed us well."

We fed on their wings until we too learned to fly under the cover of moonlight.

With the light of nuclear fire on our backs we flecked our tongues, anew.

Aghast at the lack of the morning sun. We frogs croaked in the darkness in

numbers that rival billions, we croaked in the face of infinity as

humanity just croaked. Another evolution survived for us frogs. We still mourn

the flies we eat, but only the flies.

DELUSIONS

Everybody's fine

Everybody's wonderful

Everyone's been wined and dined

Perm. Pressed

Shaved

Sheared

Thick as thieves

Pretty as pigs at the local fair

Mundane

Belated

Broken

Pasted

Clones

Drones

Bags of pretty polished bone

Everybody's fine

Everybody's wonderful

Everyone's lawns are trimmed

Groomed

Green

Fertilized with the decay of time wasted away

Laid to rot beneath the white picket fence that surrounds

the palace built on greed and the backs of the less fortunate

Everybody's fine

Everybody's wonderful

GOLD INTO GOLD INTO GOLD

Thousands of hours

Turning alcohol to piss

Still the sun doth rise

ANALYZED TO DEATH [don't overthink]

A means to an end

Means nothing without meaning

Fuck, I'm rambling

BIG PHARM [manufacture the ride]

Suffer the lonely

Spoil your company

For they too are loved by misery and no other

That's why they drown in drink

Counting their shortcomings

Their stillborn chickens

Their rotting ideals

Ideas of future and betterment have proven to be childish

Perish the thought or just perish

The result is the same

A temporary fix

Not unlike the chemical trail from prescription pad to hemoglobin train

Next stop mucus membrane

Absorb the content

Alter your mind

Manufacture the ride

THIS ISN'T LOVE

Hey ho, manipulator

Show me how you pull your strings

Sing me a smile with a silver tongue

As you pull those tendons from your teeth

Cut me open and peel me out

Crawl inside and walk about my organs

Tar-stained and whiskey soaked

Liver spotted with a drunkard's bloat

This is love

This is love

This is love

Loss is love

This is love

This is love

This is love

Blood is love

Crack open my liver

You can get drunk from my blood.

This is love.

SWARM OF THE W.A.S.P.

I look at life through ceiling fans and shit-faced grins

Perfect teeth

Accessories

Keeping up with the Jones'

Like good, White, Anglo-Saxon Protestants teach in Sunday school

Rats in a maze

Days break to save face with nothing to show for it but good measure

Oh god please!!!! Bring on the rain and wipe out all technology

Take us back to simpler times the good ol' days when blood was wine

So I can gladly fill this cup be a hero in the lush's eyes

And I feel fine.

THE GRASS IS GREENER WHERE YOU LET IT GROW [don't give up]

I've never been one to let the fun subside

But the grass is always greener on the suicide

The crossing thus far has taken 27 years 30,000 beers

And a codependent delusion of grandeur

I admire your candor, but I can't be taught

Can't be bought

Call me wicked but the things I've sought have left me wanting

Wanting more than empty bottles and endless trays of ash

I've finally found my greener grass

I've found a home beneath the grass

FREEDOM

The world will someday effervesce beneath oceans of lies and wasted seed.

Humanity will drown in greed and excess. America; the new Rome, destined

to fall, destined to hang by the neck from ropes of grandeur.

Home of the beautiful, home of the brave.

America: home of the damned. Your freedom or the illusion of such

is your death warrant. Place your hand on your heart, pledge allegiance

to naivety, now repeat after me, I am free.

BIRDS OF A FEATHER [title by Chad Pinckney]

Let's take a walk across the wire

Don't you dare look down

It'll fuck up the whole program

Take us right back to consciousness

We're not searching for a scapegoat

There's one so close to home

Where we lay in convulsions

And vomit the words that define our existence

Such a sweet blasphemy

Getting lost in a T.V. screen

Pick up where we once left off

In the belly of the beast

Comfort in gluttony

Is excess really the best?

FINITE [don't wait for tomorrow]

Waiting for the dawn

I dreamt about my deathbed

The sun never rose

FOOD CHAIN

We've scratched the surface but haven't touched the terrain

We've kept a count of all the wolves that we've slain

Left with sheep's clothing piling up in the rain.

Take heed the abundance of wool.

We found fine dining on the backs of their dead

Their constant whimpers leave their songs in your head

What once was white is now transforming to red

They're the reason your bellies are full.

Be grateful your belly is full.

OXYGEN [create/destroy]

Scared crows make attempts at murder

Their squaws scream their curses 'cross the land

Smile bright

Let's see the rust

Smile wide

Show us all the rust

Lust, love, and severed limbs leave phantom pains inside your skin

Peel your skin, scrape back the rust, carve your flesh and shed some rust

Oxidized and pickled drunk

There's a headache in my eye

I woke up in a pile of rust

When I awoke I was made of rust.

BACK TO NATURE

She donned her boots for trampling

And danced amongst the skulls

She lit a fire inside her belly

When she consumed my soul

Take me down to the old oak tree

Say your prayers and watch me swing

Inside this rope I hope to find

Some kind of inner peace

Make me a permanent necklace

Give me the will to swing

Make me a permanent necklace

So I can be set free

Make me a permanent necklace

And leave me to the trees

RECRUITS

We constructed our deathbeds from the skins of the less fortunate

Ignoring the stench of shit and happenstance that hung heavily in the air

Much to my despair

Much to my dismay

I disregard the saints that sang their praises and spit their curses

Adverse to the acceptability of human nature

Nursing deaf children to hear the word of god

Feel the spirit

Fuel the machine until it paves the way to our destruction

THE RETREAT

Withdraw!

Retreat!

Run run run

Lie a pig on high

High as a horse with acid in its eyes

Give me the gentleman's prize

Prose poetry and bloodshot skies

Restless and wicked

Am I the grifter, or grifted?

Gifted to be obliged to such ill manner

What's the matter if nothing matters?

Nothing is vibrant

So little is safe

Everything's wrong but it's all in its place

Withdraw

Retreat

Run

LIGHT

Smiles made of splinters

Strike and sliver the flesh of our unsuspecting loves

Show me passion or show me guilt

Show me the ways your fluids spill

Whilst seeing red my skin turns white

As cold and pale as the moonlight

That reflects our finite existence with every revolution

Another year past faster than the one before

Explore the dark to find the light

THE CURRENT

Lay me down on the river bed

It's my favorite place to rest my head

Tuck me in, in the rushing water

Let the current carry away my last breath

The pieces that they'll come to find on the shore

Will tell the story of the night before

Water carries silence in a way

As it carries you away

To eternal darkness or a better place

Lay me down in the river bed

HAPPINESS [is my responsibility]

Found myself to be

Miserable company

Even when alone

CELEBATE

Sharpened silver tongues

Recoil at the taste of sulfur in the air

Bless-ed are NOT the children of the millennium

Two thousand years lost in technology and reality TV

Click thy tongue minister

Spit thine lie

Curs-ed art though for refraining from the heavy stench of cunt

That hangs in confession booths across nations

Good night Minister Sinister

THE CURSE

I dug my teeth out from the trench

I cursed the moon with clenched fists and fresh spit

Howling over the hum of the atomic chain that held us together

In that moment so brief

Fleet

I dug myself from the trenches using nothing but my teeth

With acid on my tongue she spoke to me

Did I curse the Moon?

...Or perhaps did she curse me?

DANCE LIKE ME

But of course

I'm high as a horse

Happy as a clam

I can dance to this

Like american bandstand

Take my hand

I'll show you the way

Today's topic the woman in black

Back from the top serving Hell A la Carte

Plain and simple If I get an acquittal

I'll wither and rot

Talking shit on God

Waiting for the day that I can move along

I pine for the other side

COCK FIGHT

"Give 'em what for!" My lady said

With venom on her breath

Before they broke my head on the corner of Windsor

"Whatcha in for?" Beelzebub asked

Pulling a nail from my back

With his hands full of splinters

"They called it love" I tried to reply

Over thousands of cries of the broken and wanting

"I died for what the damned call love"

THE MISSIONARY

Enter the Predator

Spitting etiquette

Spewing prose

Exit reason

Abandon all logic

Collectively Chaotic

Curtain call

A brave new world of bastards and butchers

Cunts and consumers

Laughing from their dead eyes

Much to my surprise

Much to my chagrin

There's no sign of an ending

Here's hoping for an ending

Enter the predator

ALL IS WELL [just breathe]

Anxiety strikes

I can taste it in my throat

Don't forget to breathe

THE MATCH

I could watch the fire

For hours if you'll let me

Don't be put out

FLUB OF MY LIFE

Once upon a one night stand

I found happily never after

In a wastebasket lined with contraceptives

Full of a million bastards

And all I think about is you

Reddening my hands

And giving into drink

I think it kind of funny

Just how hard it is to think

Now that there's poison in the water

And stains upon the sheets

TODAY IS THE DAY

The silence of substance abuse carries beauty in a way

A wayward bus

Days slip away

Sniffing and sipping

Smoking and spitting

Killing the body to quiet the brain

All smiles

All hopeful

All for tomorrow

But today keeps repeating

The smiles are receding

I guess there's always tomorrow

I hope I make it to tomorrow

LASSO THE MOON

In the light of the harvest moon I digress

I insist we must endure

Robotic in reason

Relinquished, defeated

A refusal of faith

An itching for lust

Scratching and biting at air

Deny damnation

Gather your saints

Chew on your prescription pills

Gather the harvest it's looking like rain

I order you bring me the moon

TEETH

"It's raining teeth", said the chimney sweep

as the porcelain pelted the streets

paved with soiled sheets and discarded candor

No matter

Never mind

Don't speak

Through broken umbrellas the sky starts to bite

"Look at my collection of new pearly whites",

said the sweep with his hands full of teeth.

LIFE SPAN [liver failure]

Call me the "barfly on the wall"

Watching the world through the dirty windows of dirty public houses across this great tattered nation

Measuring time in empty glasses and rapidly filling ashtrays

"Bar keep, let's do that again."

Exercising the right to exorcise the light

Call me the "barfly on the wall"

MINISTER SHIVER [wolf in sheep's clothing]

Sleep

Scourge

Binge

Purge

Withered and festered

May the children be bless-ed

Good things will come to the Nihilist who holds his tongue

Hey Mister!

Come hither

She's starting to shiver

Sleep

Scourge

Binge

Purge

LET ME IN

Whether closed doors or closed minds

Someone will always be shut out

Barricades built on fear and bad bloodlines

Open your doors

Open your minds

There's beauty out there if you care enough to find it

Open your eyes to the grandeur

It's yours for the taking

Open your hearts

Open your doors

Let love in

RAT MAN

You may find me hanging from the roots of my teeth

You may find buried beneath the roots of a tree

You may find me growing on the wrong side of the weeds

Growing death and mold and fester

Let the Vermin feed

My body feeds the rats

The rats they feed the fleas

The fleas carry the plague

Sent to cleanse humanity

If life is but a cycle

Then it's time to break the track

You can read my time of exit by the boils on my back

My body feeds the rats

The rats they feed the fleas

The worst things that can plague a man

Are the vermin he can't see.

CPSIA information can be obtained
at www.ICGtesting.com
Printed in the USA
FSHW020010190721
83338FS

9 798715 995643